PUPPETEER

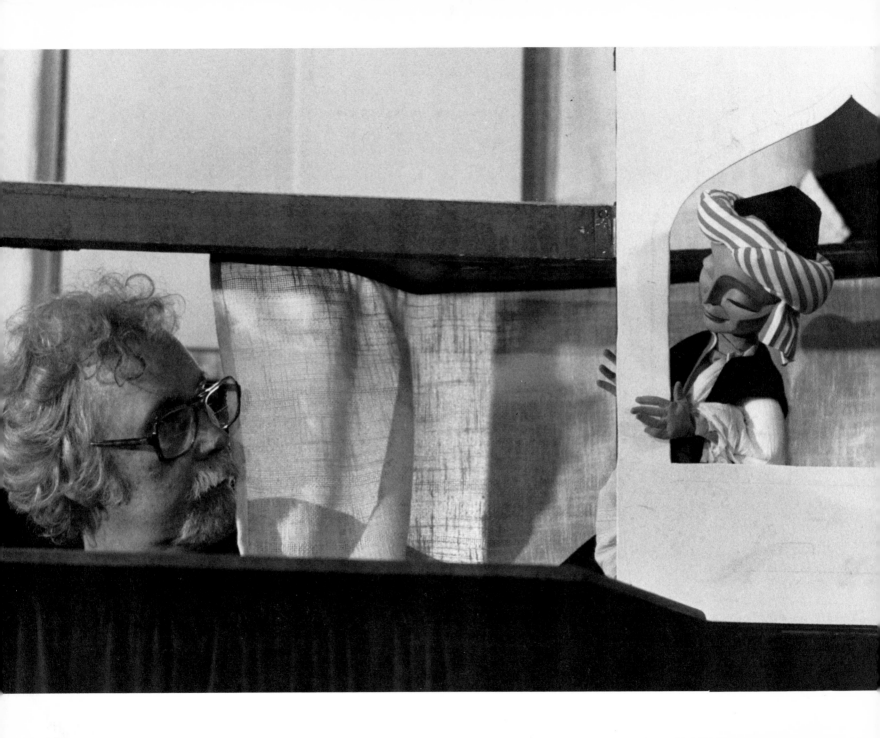

PUPPETEER

By Kathryn Lasky

Photographs by Christopher G. Knight

Macmillan Publishing Company

New York

Macmillan Publishing Company
866 Third Avenue, New York, N.Y. 10022
Collier Macmillan Canada, Inc.
Printed in the United States of America
10   9   8   7   6   5   4   3   2   1

Library of Congress Cataloging in Publication Data
Lasky, Kathryn.
Puppeteer.
Summary: Text and photographs follow Paul Vincent
Davis, a professional hand puppeteer, as he mounts a
production of Aladdin and His Wonderful Lamp.
1. Davis, Paul Vincent—Juvenile literature.
2. Puppets and puppet-plays—Juvenile literature.
[1. Puppet plays   2. Davis, Paul Vincent] I. Knight,
Christopher G., ill.   II. Title.
PN1982.D3L3   1985   791.5'3'0924   84-42987
ISBN 0-02-751660-1

We would like to thank Claire DeMeo for helping us begin this book, and all the staff of the Puppet Show Place for their patience while we were working on it. Funding for production of Aladdin and His Wonderful Lamp was provided by WBZ Friends for the Arts and the National Endowment for the Arts.

—K. L. and C. G. K.

A VANISHING PALACE

Paul Vincent Davis is a man with problems. He has to figure out how to move forty slaves leading camels, who in turn are leading elephants carrying basins brimful with jewels, across a stage measuring 3½ by 2 feet. Before an audience's eyes, he has to make a palace appear to float in the air from Persia to Africa and back again. He must turn a dwarf into a magician and create a magical garden with an orchard of trees that bear jewels instead of fruit.

For all of these problems, Paul alone must invent the solutions, and then, with his own hands, he must make them work. For he is a puppeteer, and this is his job—solving problems, magical or otherwise, that are part of the tales he dramatizes through his puppets at the Puppet Show Place in Boston. The tale that he plans to stage next will be the most challenging he has ever encountered. It is the story of Aladdin and his wonderful lamp.

For most of his life Paul has planned, produced, and performed puppet shows. Some days he takes his shows to the people—to schools, theaters, and museums—but on most days people come to him at the Puppet Show Place. They might see Rumplestiltskin spinning straw into gold, or *The Leprechaun of Donegal*, in which, as if by magic, a cornstalk grows from a puppet's head. Behind the magical performances lie artistry, will, and Paul's special kind of daring that makes him want to do everything himself—from making the puppets to the mechanical engineering of the tricks to the performance itself. To be a puppeteer is to be engineer, seamstress, set designer, and actor, all at once.

A HAND PUPPETEER

"This is not a doll. It is a puppet," Paul says as he holds up a princess from a past show. "Only when you put your hand in it does it come to life." The puppet begins to move slightly. She puts one tiny hand to her cheek and tilts her head. Instantly she appears worried. *"Oh dear! Dear beast, how I love you!"* She extends the hands up a bit and taps her temple with a finger. *"Let me think."* Then Paul collapses her on his other arm in a sleeping position. By expanding and contracting ever so slightly his controlling hand inside the puppet, he makes the princess appear to rise and sink in the rhythmic breathing of sleep.

In puppetry, illusions of feeling, posture, and mood are instantly created through a few deft movements of the hand. As Paul is walking down a street or waiting in line at the supermarket, he frequently catches himself making small hand movements—finger exercises or wrist motions that would make a puppet seem to be looking for a pin on the ground, or listening, or feeling frustrated, or experiencing any one of a million different attitudes or gestures. In puppeteering, all life and feeling are contained within and expressed through the movement of the human hand. This is what makes a puppet appear to live.

Most hand puppeteers would rather work alone, which is why they prefer puppets to marionettes. A single marionette requires two hands to operate it, but a puppet requires just one. That leaves a hand free for another puppet, and with two puppets there can be a show, an entire world created and controlled by one single person. "I, too, can be a handsome prince!" Paul says almost gleefully, although he resembles more a portly king. The one rule is that there can be only two active puppets on stage at any single moment. But voices can be heard off stage from other characters; music can be played by activating a cassette player with a foot control. Scenery can be changed when one puppet exits and a hand is free. Lights can be dimmed or raised by a free foot or a spare hand.

"Maybe all hand puppeteers were just bossy kids and never outgrew it, but we do like to control," Paul admits. And they are in total control of that world they have created within the black-draped aperture of the puppet stage.

Paul began over forty years ago, when he was ten years old, in his family's garage in Virginia. He started with two real puppets, a bunch of stuffed animals, some borrowed dolls, and a makeshift stage constructed out of orange crates and old sheets. He had decided to give a performance of *Cinderella* for the neighborhood children. The children did not like the show. All through the performance they complained: "Look, you can see his head." "Look, there're his hands." "I saw his whole shoulder." "Look, there are his feet under the sheet." "This is dumb."

Paul didn't think it was dumb. He just became more determined to do it better. His father built him a real stage, and Paul kept practicing.

THE WORKROOM UPSTAIRS

Behind all the magical effects—the illusions that come to life on the puppet stage—is a very unmagical place where productions are planned, developed, and built. It is a workroom, two actually, not backstage, but above the stage, for Paul lives right over the Puppet Show Place. This is the place where puppets are made and repaired. There are shelves with molds of puppet heads labeled *Beast, Sorcerer, Rumple S. S., Prince, Frog, Stepmom*. Scenery is also built in this room, so fragments of painted cardboard are everywhere. Most important, there are the puppets. Hanging lifeless, their faces brightly glazed, they wait like actors who can never take off their makeup.

Paul and a helper sew all the costumes for the puppets. There are boxes filled with tiny hands, each finger exquisitely sewn and ready to be attached to a small sleeve. Other boxes hold fabric, each with intriguing labels like *Phake Phur, Pseudo Suede/Real Suede, Heavy Leather, Glitzy Tulle, Glitz, Chiffon, Gauze, Soft and Drapey*. There are spools and darning eggs. Still more boxes are filled with tacks, buttons, and odd metal or plastic pieces that are used not just for sewing but for sound effects—to anything from storms to fires. One box is labeled *Treasure Chest Noises* and another *Troll Show*. In addition to the sketches for costumes, props are scattered about — miniature wishing wells, wheelbarrows, ships, treasure chests, and cobbler's benches. In these two workrooms Paul will build the jeweled orchards, the vanishing palaces, the caravans of slaves and elephants, and the puppets that will enact *Aladdin and His Wonderful Lamp*.

SEARCHING FOR ALADDIN

The plot, adapted from the *Thousand and One Nights*, is simple enough: In Bagdad, a boy lives with his widowed mother. They are very poor. He meets a man who claims to be his uncle. But the man is really an evil magician who wants a magic lamp hidden deep in an underground cave. The magician gets the boy to retrieve the lamp through magic tricks and deceit. When the magician admits his true identity, the boy suddenly refuses to hand over the magic lamp, and the magician seals him in the cave. The boy soon discovers the djinn (or genie) of the lamp, escapes, becomes rich, marries the sultan's daughter, loses her to the magician, gets her back, and lives happily ever after.

That is the plot, but it is not the whole story. It does not convey the bustle in the streets, the magnificence of the palaces, and the nature of the nine principal characters: Aladdin, his Mother, the Dwarf/Magician, the Sultan, the Princess, the Princess's Servant, a Royal Herald, a Rug Merchant, and the Djinn. In early summer, Paul begins by reading many versions of the tale. In one, Aladdin is described as a vicious, nasty boy, in another as a lazy, thoughtless one. But Paul is not satisfied with the notion of a good-for-nothing kid winding up with buckets of gold.

a line with a harder edge. Around him on his work-table are many books on Persian and Oriental art. He opens one and studies a miniature painting with jewellike colors. It shows men, their faces the shape of long O's, with neatly trimmed beards and curved mustaches. Their eyes are the shape of plump fish—tilted fish swimming at steep angles. There is a flatness to their faces. Everything exists within the same plane without shadows, hollows, or dimples. He begins to revise his sketches and moves toward these simpler forms for faces.

"It is not just like looking at a jewel, but being inside the jewel." Paul is looking at another book now, one on Islamic architecture. He has come across a dazzling series of photographs of mosque domes. Some are sheathed in gold leaf and are inlaid with jewels and precious stones. He soon realizes that for this show he will need a case of gold paint, and he might actually use up the entire contents of his glitz box with all its fake jewels and sequins and gold braid. After all, there are two palaces to build, and a jeweled orchard.

For a month Paul has been going through books on Persian and Oriental art and architecture studying paintings of people, plants, animals, clothing. The paintings have a unique perspective, an intriguing flatness, that has given Paul an idea. His production of *Aladdin and His Wonderful Lamp* will

One of Paul's earliest decisions about the play is to make the boy poor, hard working, but unable to find a job. As Paul thinks about the characters he starts to sketch them. He draws several versions of all the puppets, especially Aladdin and the Sultan. He is not altogether pleased with the rounded, bulbous nose of the Sultan and the cartoon look of some of the characters. He begins to move toward

have a large cast of nonspeaking characters that, as hand puppets, would be impossible to move around the stage. Inspired by the work of medieval Persian artists, Paul decides to make them flat, actually cut out from plywood and painted. Major puppets such as Aladdin and his Mother will, of course, be full-bodied, regular hand puppets. But the forty slaves, the elephants, the camels that must march across the stage in the dazzling procession will be "flats" cut out with an electric jigsaw. Immediately, Paul closes up the book and dashes out to his favorite hardware store to buy a jigsaw. That night he experiments with the saw, cutting all sorts of shapes.

The flatness becomes for Paul a key mechanical element in the design of the show. The city streets will be on flat pieces that can be lifted away to show a barren desert. The Sultan's palace will appear flat, but its two central doors will swing open to reveal a jeweled interior. Landscapes, cityscapes, and buildings will be illustrated on flat surfaces that will be able to lift, open, or slide—three basic movements to reveal other spaces and interiors. A stage plan has started to form in Paul's mind, and he has a clever idea. When the rock to the cave entrance must magically flip or slide away, Paul is considering using a puff of smoke. It is a handy device that he has used before to mask a trick.

By midsummer Paul knows how the scenery will change, which puppets will be flats, and which will be full bodied. He knows what alterations he must make to his puppet stage, and he has written thirteen pages of a script on his word-processor. It is a beginning, he tells a friend, but there are still too many puffs of smoke.

By the end of the summer there has been progress. Paul has figured out how, at the Magician's bidding, the rock to the cave will open on a special pivoting hinge. He knows more about Aladdin's character. "He's a nice kid but not too nice—no Goody Two-Shoes. A little bit pushy, but full of humor."

And he has a completed script. There are twenty-eight pages of dialogue and a special role for him as al-Hariri. Al-Hariri was an actual historical figure, one of Arabia's foremost storytellers. As al-Hariri he will tell the tale of Aladdin and occasionally make appearances in front of the puppet stage in a turban and flowing gown. But there is something missing from this script. Paul has written words for the nine major characters, but he has yet to find voices for each of them. They must all sound very different in spite of the fact that all nine voices come from one throat—Paul's.

MAKING THE PUPPETS

A violinist does not make his own violin, but a puppeteer often does make his or her own puppets. It is early fall now, and the leaves have started to turn colors outside the window by Paul's worktable. In front of him is a glass jar filled with small balls of modeling clay. He takes one and presses it onto a larger ball of clay. He has been doing this for almost twenty minutes. To his left is a piece of paper with a rough sketch of a face.

Occasionally he glances at the sketch. Nearby is an art book open to a page showing paintings of the faces he has been studying. Soon the ball of clay is large enough and smooth enough. Paul reaches for a flat wooden tool and scoops out half a moon for an eye. He works on the eyes for a while and then begins to pull out a nose. As the face emerges from the ball of clay, Paul often pauses to hold it up to the light coming in through the window. He turns and dips and rotates the head in the column of morning sunlight. Shadows slide across the face, and the dull clay eyes, still unfinished, appear to open and shut. It is an illusion, of course, as light and shadow play across the dramatic planes and hollows of the face.

Nothing about the facial features is intended to be realistic. The size of the heads, the angles of their faces, the proportion of features have all been exaggerated so they will project across the puppet stage to a roomful of people and best catch the light that will animate their faces during a performance. Unlike a doll, which can sit on a shelf and look almost alive, a puppet is supposed to seem real only when manipulated by the puppeteer. Without the puppeteer's skill, it is simply an inanimate object—a stuffed sock with button eyes, a sculpted head glazed bright with paints.

By the end of the month, nine clay heads have been sculpted. Paul will make plaster molds from each of them and from the molds will cast thirteen heads. This is because he will need not one Aladdin, but at least four, and not one Mother but two, as well as two Magicians. There must be duplicate heads for some characters, because it is easier to change puppets entirely than to change a single puppet's costume. Aladdin is transformed from a poor boy in rags to merchant to prince. The fourth Aladdin will be a marionette mounted on horseback and wearing the rich cloak of a merchant. When he goes to search for his lost Princess toward the end of the play, he must ride his horse across "the northern mountains, the western desert, and the southern sea."

Aladdin's Mother also changes costume, her tattered veils becoming silken ones with threads of gold and silver. The Magician changes entirely, first appearing as a dwarf through powerful sorcery, then as his true evil self. Both Dwarf and Magician are the same puppet, but in order for the Dwarf to change, as if by magic, into the Magician, he must be a trick puppet mounted on a rod. A bundle carried by the Dwarf will conceal the Magician's head until the transformation. The second Magician used in later scenes will look identical to the first but will be a simple hand puppet—no tricks, no dwarfs hidden inside, just evil.

With the nine heads sculpted, Paul is ready to begin making molds. Using old cardboard cartons, he will pour liquid plaster of paris around each sculpted head until its impression is cast. The clay head of Fatima, the Princess's Servant, is the first to be immersed in the milky plaster sea. She must sit there quietly with the plaster up to her ears for one hour until it sets. Then, after rubbing the exposed part of her face with a soap solution, Paul fills the box entirely with plaster. He will let the mold set for several hours, separate the two parts, remove the clay head, and put the parts of the mold in the oven to bake at a very low temperature until they are completely dry. This process must be repeated nine times. During all this sitting and

watching and baking, Paul often sketches ideas for costumes or tries out different voices in his search for each character's sound. Even as the other clay heads wait to be plunged into the plaster sea, Paul cannot resist wrapping strips of paper towel around their heads for a turban or draping the Princess with an old dishcloth secured by a circlet of plastic pearls for a crown.

These odd arrangements and improvisations of homely things might look like rags and tags, bits and pieces, but they feed Paul's imagination and will become transformed through his artistry into a special kind of magic. Months later, in a darkened theater, they will make children and grownups hold their breaths, laugh, maybe cry, gasp, look again and, for forty-five minutes, suspend disbelief as they watch *Aladdin and His Wonderful Lamp.*

Two days later Paul patches any nicks or pock-marks and bands the two parts of the plaster molds together tightly. Then he pours a liquid-rubber casting compound through the small hole at the base of each mold. It will take eight hours for the rubber to dry, becoming a hollow duplicate of the original clay head. When removed, the heads are light, weighing a few ounces at the most, so that Paul's hands will not grow tired. The neck of each of the puppets is large enough for two of Paul's fingers, so he can move the head easily.

So far it has taken Paul a summer and fall to develop the characters in his mind, give them speech, and, finally, features. He has had the usual interruptions. One week he got the flu. Then he had to pack up *Beauty and the Beast* and fly to Toronto for three performances. Another week he staged *The Leprechaun of Donegal* in Washington, D.C., then *Seneca Indian Tales* in western Massachusetts. During Christmas it was round-the-clock *Beauty and the Beast*, a Christmas favorite at the Puppet Show Place. Finally, in the middle of January a blizzard started up and everything stopped—airplanes, schools, performances. Everything, that is, except Paul. All during the blizzard, as the world got whiter and whiter, inside Paul's studio things became more colorful as he painted the rubber heads.

Painting a puppet's face is very similar to apply-

ing the heavy theatrical makeup of an actor. First, Paul mixes a base coat for the flesh tone and paints the entire head. Then he begins to add the color and shadowing that will reinforce the lines and contours of the face he has sculpted. It should not appear too flat under the strong stage lighting. As Paul paints the rubber head, it seems to be gathering the facial muscle and tone for its role. The head is becoming a puppet, one that will deliver its lines with expression and sometimes passion, in spite of the fact that its face is frozen forever into a single expression that is neither quite joy nor sorrow.

Paul has many makeup tricks. A touch of red on the outer part of the brow bone as well as a dot of red in the inner corner of the eye gives a youthful, lively look to the puppet's face. Its lips stand out when the lower lip is outlined with a darker color and filled in with a lighter one. The procedure is then reversed on the upper lip. "I learned that by watching a TV commercial for lipstick. But here's one they don't do on TV." Paul draws a thin black line between the upper and lower lip. "Strictly for puppets. It makes them look as if they are talking."

The black crescent shape varies on each puppet in accordance with the eye contour that Paul has sculpted. The evil Magician's eyes are two black slashes. The Rug Merchant's eyes are like half moons, whereas the Royal Herald's eyes are slivered crescents of a new moon. Aladdin's Mother's eyes are as sleek as dolphins in their shape.

Paul begins to paint the head's eye spaces. When finished, the eyes will not have pupils or lashes. Instead, they will be black crescents, giving the puppet a blind look from close up. From the audience, however, the puppets will not look blind at all. The audience will assume that the puppets have lifelike eyes, as a person, seeing another from a distance and unable to see each feature of the eyes, never doubts that the eyes are there.

As Paul finishes painting each head, he places it on a stand and drapes it with swatches of the various fabrics he is considering using for the costumes. He winds the swatches into turbans, lets them fall as veils or burnooses, or wraps them as simple peasant scarves. From the glitz box he takes a pendant and pins it to the Princess's veil so that the stars of the fake diamonds and sapphires rest in the middle of her forehead. A child's bracelet of dark enameled beads circles the Mother's head. Close up, the puppets look overly made up and very artificial. But Paul scoots back in his rolling chair to view them. He is trying to imagine them on the small stage under theatrical lighting. Paul squints his eyes to focus better, and just as his own eyes become slits for his imagination, he sneezes. It is a huge sneeze from a very large man. The room seems to quake. Twelve puppet heads tremble on their poles. Turbans quiver. Veils flutter, "diamonds" shimmer. Light and dark shadows race across their faces, and he can almost hear the muffled voices deep in their rubber throats trying to escape. For that brief second the puppets are not facsimiles of life at all. They are actors waiting for their voices, their movement, waiting like the rest of us for that little slit between two eternities that is called life. Their lives will be played on the 3½- by 2-foot stage.

HALFWAY THERE

In the early spring Paul calls Eleanor Boylan, an old friend who is also a puppeteer. He has consulted with Eleanor throughout the fall and winter on the show. It is Eleanor who will direct Paul in the rehearsals. There is no way a puppeteer can see how the puppets look to the audience from where he or she stands. Every puppeteer needs a director to sit out where the audience will be and tell him or her where a gesture, a move, a tone misses or hits the mark. Eleanor will do this for Paul.

They begin with dummy puppets by figuring out the moves, the various stage actions, how to get one puppet off and another on, how to rotate the scenery from desert to city to desert with one hand while having a puppet on the other. In the evenings when Paul is not "staging" with Eleanor, he continues to work on scenery and other props. Caravans of camels and elephants, processions of slaves bearing basins of jewels, and entire bazaars cut out of ⅛-inch plywood will be painted and parts jointed to make the "flats"—those one-dimensional lifescapes of animals and people—suggesting the vitality and bustle of life in an ancient world.

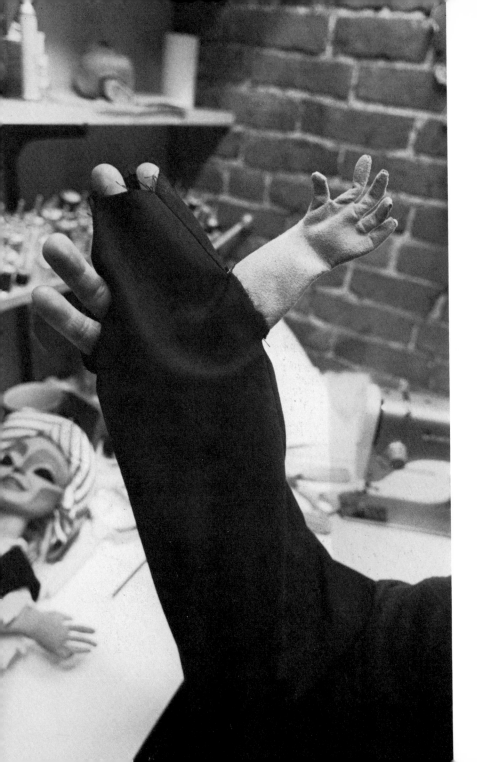

In addition to making flats, Paul has been building the bodies of the puppets, for although their heads have been made and painted they have as yet no hands or feet or torsos. Tiny puppet hands measuring about 2½ inches long are cut out of Ultrasuede and sewn. Many puppets have hands like mittens, but each of Paul's puppets has ten separate fingers. Pipe cleaners are inserted into the fingers and bent to humanlike positions. Thirty little hands and one hundred fifty tiny fingers must be made for this puppet show alone. The puppets' feet are also made from Ultrasuede. Fishing weights are inserted to help the feet swing and move as if they are really walking. The underbody of a puppet is a dark, funnel-shaped sleeve with a ring at the bottom. Its costume will be made to fit not just the puppet but also the distance from the puppet's head to Paul's elbow. In this way no part of Paul's arm will be visible as the puppet walks, dances, stumbles, swishes, swirls, or jumps across the stage.

"Not shiny enough," the young woman says.

"Could we hit it with a little bit of gold paint?" Paul asks.

"We don't want to cover that bright red bead."

"How about this?" Paul asks, taking a flat silver medallion with filigree from the box labeled *glitz*. "We could spray that with gold."

"Yeah. And probably jewel it, too."

"Yes."

Paul and Karen Larsen, a professional costume designer and seamstress, are discussing the costume of the Royal Herald. Paul has designed all of the costumes and sewn some, but this show is so big he has called in Karen to help. "Look," says Paul, "the Herald, he's sort of ordinary but he does work for royalty. He has to look rich but not as fancy as the Sultan."

"We've got to find something really glitzy," Karen says.

"And outrageous," Paul adds. "The Herald is a kind of clown. . . . *'Everyone inside! Everyone inside!'*" Paul slips into a high-pitched voice and continues. " *'The Princess is going to her baths. Close all the doors and windows. No one must see the Princess.'* " The voice belongs to the Herald, a character who is not too bright and spends most of his time rushing about trying to sound important. "Aaah! Here's something!" Paul exclaims in his own voice now. He pulls out a pendant dripping heavily with beads. "Perfectly ugly jewelry that some lady once wore!" he sighs.

Most of the costume jewelry in the glitz box Paul has picked up at rummage sales and second-hand shops. He also has several yards of glittery braid as well as gold and silver tassels. "Glitz" is a word that pops up often in Paul and Karen's conversations. For them it suggests something that is both fancy and glittery, ritzy and glossy—"glitz." And for this show full of magic and Oriental splendor, rich gowns, and jeweled caves, glitz is very important. In the darkened puppet theater, when the lights grow dim, the glitz must glow. If the puppet is royal, or rich, or both, the costume will be laced with gold threads or edged with silver or iced with sequins and glitter or trimmed with feathers. Paul has written in the script that the rich were indeed so rich that "gold dripped from their clothes as honey from honeycombs." The poor characters such as Aladdin and his Mother in the beginning of the story do not have two sequins to rub together. But as his fortune grows Aladdin's wardrobe becomes more glitzy.

Paul's first costume decision concerned what colors each character should wear. Even as some of the characters' clothes change from rags to riches, the colors will remain the same. Aladdin's colors are red, white, and black. As his fortune changes, the fabrics will change from red cotton and black felt to red and black satin. The Mother's costume will be black with touches of purple, the Princess's shades of blue and lavender, and the Sultan's a deep red.

"We have to find a nasty color for the Magician," Karen says. She and Paul settle on a green velour fabric. It's a color that never came from nature—an electric green, bright and harsh.

The Djinn is a rod puppet that extends over six feet in height and has a soft, sculptured face of gold lamé. He will have a cascade of flowing red for his robe, similar to China silk but more durable.

In all, thirteen different costumes must be designed and sewn. The seams are shorter for puppet costumes but the process is longer, because it is harder to work in this smaller scale. "But there are advantages," Karen points out as she stitches on the decorative edging of the Herald's cloak. "The puppets are always here. You don't have to call them in for fittings. You can glue clothes to them, staple things on them. They never complain. They never gain weight at Christmas, either."

Handmade earrings of thread, strung with pearly beads, sequins, and fake sapphires, are glued to the Princess's ears. A small "emerald" encircled with "diamonds" glitters from the Magician's finger. In addition to all these trimmings, the costumes' underpinnings must be sewn. Live actors wait in the wings for their cues, but these puppet actors hang upside down on hooks, waiting for Paul's hand to slip into the underbody sleeve, flip them upright, and put them in motion. When a puppet is flipped, the costume must fall in place. All the layers of cloaks and gowns and robes must hang straight and not become tangled. But they must also be able to move on the stage, to swish and swirl, to drape

properly and shake free at the right moment. This movement will make the puppets appear more lively, yet it must be controllable. The controls in this case are "swing tacks," which are small chains of stitches forming strings between the various layers so that a cloak will be able to swirl but not to the point of getting tangled or knocking a prop off a table. Each layer of clothing has a set of swing tacks that prevent it from dropping over the puppet's head when hung upside down, insuring that the costumes will move with balletic grace but never swing out of control.

For four weeks Paul and Karen labor over the costumes. One afternoon they make a "glitz trip" downtown and come back with over one hundred dollars' worth of new braids, tassels, jewels, and feathers. A group of tiny "silk" pillows are sewn and "embroidered" for the Princess's settee. An ordinary egg cup becomes a wine goblet when it is glued with lace and beads, then sprayed gold.

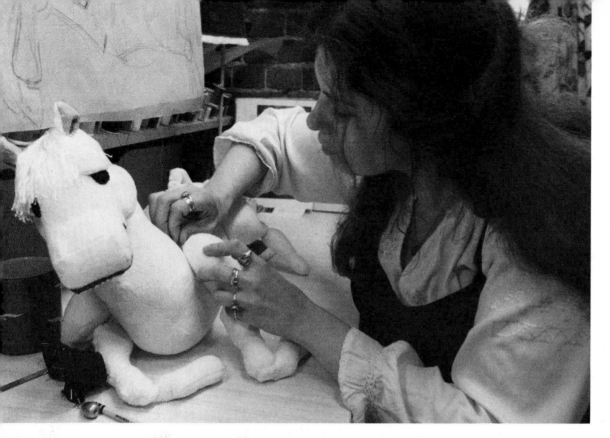 

Paul paints a miniature Oriental rug that is three inches wide and four inches long for the Rug Merchant in the bazaar to carry over his arm. A soft, sculptured white horse cut from a handmade pattern is stuffed and sewn to take Aladdin on his search for the lost Princess, after the evil Magician has whisked her away.

Paul works late into the spring nights. Caves are painted, sets built that flip like pages from deserts to palaces. A tiny jeweled crown for the Princess is made. The mechanism for turning the Dwarf puppet into the evil Magician is worked out. The Dwarf is mounted on a rod and will enter carrying his large bundle on his head. There will be a burble of magic words. The invisible rod will stab upward as drawstrings on top of the bundle are loosened. The bundle drops open in a quick spill of electric green, and the evil Magician's head pops up. His cloak, which was formerly the lining of the Dwarf's bundle, now hides the Dwarf beneath it. The Dwarf's bundle has been turned inside out to produce the Magician.

COMING TO LIFE

The puppets have been made, costumes sewn, props gathered, and the scenery constructed. There are a few minor details left to do. The palace that Aladdin builds for his Princess has indeed been built, but Paul has not gotten around to painting it. One bag of gold has been misplaced, but it will turn up. A turban or two still need feathers, but aside from these minor chores everything is ready for rehearsal.

The cold, wet season that New England calls spring has actually grown warm. It is mid-May now, and there are daffodils the size of golden goblets outside Paul's workroom window. Little cat-faced pansies tumble colorfully in window boxes, and lilies of the valley push out of the earth. But Paul sees none of the color of this bright May morning. He is downstairs in the theater of the Puppet Show Place. Heavy black curtains are drawn across the entrance, and a hand-written note pinned to the curtains reads: QUIET—REHEARSAL IN PROGRESS.

Inside, the theater is dark except for the stage, which is brightly lit. On the extreme right (or stage left) is Aladdin's house, which is a shabby, cracked-stucco-looking building with a large window. On a higher level in the center of the stage is the royal palace. On the extreme left (or stage right) is an elegant building—the royal baths where the Princess will come to bathe.

Eleanor Boylan is sitting in the fourth row. "Are you going to try to 'go,' Paul, or just read it this time?"

"Go," Paul says.

He disappears behind the stage. Eleanor calls, "Ready—ta da! Da da! Ra da! Ta da!" She produces a tooth-rattling, tongue-flipping fanfare, calling out, "Toots! Cymbals! Drum rolls!" to a nonexistent orchestra. Paul whirls out from behind the stage, shaking a tambourine with a score of streamers.

He fixes the audience of two with his pale blue eyes. He is a different man entirely—his posture, his gait, his voice are now "in character." He has become the Arabian storyteller.

"I am al-Hariri, a—" His tongue gets caught on "al-Hariri." "Uh-oh, I blew it." He starts again. "I am al-Hariri, a teller of tales, spinner of dreams, and a sculptor with words. I'll tell you the tale of Aladdin and his wonderful lamp. It happened a thousand years ago . . . in the city of Bagdad, a city of a thousand merchants. They sold rugs and rags and relishes. There were potters, porters, peddlers, tanners, tinners, tailors, butchers, bakers, and beggars."

The first run-through is not great. Paul forgets a lot of his lines, and Eleanor must prompt him often. Eleanor has many suggestions—Aladdin must walk faster, the Princess must never turn her back on the Magician, the puppets are tilted too far back and must bow forward for audience contact. The Princess, a tantalizing cloud of lavender, must enter more slowly so the audience can relish her; and her plump servant, Fatima, with a voice like sandpaper on harp strings, must waddle a bit slower.

Paul and Eleanor go over some of the difficult scenes again. Paul removes the stage curtains, which usually hide him from the audience, so he can see the puppets better. The first scene—where Aladdin returns dejected after a day of being unable to find work—needs polishing. This is where the Magician makes his entrance pretending to be Aladdin's uncle.

MOTHER: *Aladdin, have you found work, my son?*
ALADDIN: *No, Mother. No one would take time to talk to me. The seller of rugs said I was only fit to be a beggar.*

The Mother comforts Aladdin; then, looking dejected, he exits so Paul can take him off his hand and get the Magician on.

MOTHER: *Poor Aladdin. What is to become of us? But it is late. I must go and prepare supper.*
MAGICIAN [enters]: *This has to be the place. I followed him through the streets. He must live here in this miserable place.*

Eleanor jumps up and interrupts. "Paul, have the Magician really swish that cape—super swish here. It punctuates his evilness. And when Aladdin comes back onstage, try having him sit leaning against the house. That way he can slump and look really dejected."

MAGICIAN: *You, there, young man.*
ALADDIN: *Yes, sir.*
MAGICIAN: *Can you direct me to the home of Mustaffa, the tailor?*
ALADDIN: *Sir, this is the place you seek.*

Paul's own expression changes instantly to match the mood of each character as he speaks the lines, but an audience would never see these expressions with the curtains in place. Eleanor concentrates instead on the body language of the puppets and what it says to her out in the empty theater. Sometimes she is in the front row, sometimes the back, but most often it is the second or third row where she sits. It is from here that Eleanor can judge the scope of their movements—when a gesture is not large enough, a posture off, a walk too fast or too slow.

Three times during the first rehearsal she has called out to Paul, "Super swish!" It has always been in reference to the Magician's green cape. By the following week Paul has the super swishes down pat. He needs less prompting, but he is still forgetting to put the cave cutouts on the stage when the scene changes from Bagdad to the desert. Without them, there is no lamp for Aladdin to discover!

This week Eleanor is sitting in the front row. Just off to her right, between the stage and the first row, is a young man sitting at a table with an odd assortment of gear. Some of it looks musical. There is a harmonium on the table, an autoharp, a guitar, a conga drum. But there is also a coffee can with a small piece of wood inside that has been strung taut like a bow, two wooden, rectangular blocks, and a tin box that was the lining of an old refrigerator from Ohio. The man on the stool is John Lewandowski. He is a musician and puppeteer himself, and he and Paul have worked together on several shows, designing music. Paul tells him the effects he wants and John composes—often on the spot. Today is their first music run-through. John will make music for *Aladdin and His Wonderful Lamp* with everything from the refrigerator box to Tibetan prayer bells. There will be the thin, fragile sounds of a recorder as well as the manic chatter of wooden castanets. Eventually, the music will be recorded on a cassette that Paul will control backstage.

Eleanor and Paul run through the show two more times. The pacing of the Princess's entrance is just right now. The delicate recorder music played when Aladdin and the Princess first speak is perfect. The scene that needs work now is the one in which

Aladdin's Mother goes to the Sultan to ask for the Princess's hand in marriage for her son. She carries with her a chest of jewels which Aladdin, now in possession of the lamp, has demanded from the Djinn. The lamp has made them rich. The Mother is still dressed in black and purple, but through her gown run threads of gold and silver and a scattering of sequins. It is the second Mother puppet, the rich one, who goes to court on her son's behalf.

SULTAN: *Good morning. What can I do for you, my good woman?*
MOTHER: *Sire . . . I . . . uh . . . promise me that you will forgive me in advance for what I am about to ask.*

Eleanor interrupts. "Paul, have her really scrape the floor in front of him. Collapse, you know, in humbleness and fear at his feet." The mother suddenly drops. The folds of her gown nearly swallow her entirely.

SULTAN: *Ha-ha. A strange request, but very well! I promise to forgive you for asking, but I do not promise to do what you ask.*
MOTHER: *Sire, my son has sent these trinkets as a gift for the Princess. He asks that she may be his wife.*
SULTAN: *Wife? Wife to your miserable son! I should have his head cut off!*

Eleanor: "Head down, Paul. She should be shaking now. Sobbing!"
The Sultan looms large and crimson in his jewel-encrusted robes. The Mother is a trembling heap of black veils on the floor at his feet. Backstage, the action is just as dramatic. With the Mother puppet on his left hand and the Sultan on his right, Paul's face is sliding through hundreds of expressions. He simpers and scowls. His eyes flash with anger, his mouth crumples in despair, and his chin quivers. Even as the Mother is opening her chest of jewels— which is not an easy maneuver for the puppet to execute—Paul keeps the dramatic intensity going.

SULTAN: *These jewels are magnificent. I have never seen the like of these in my life. . . . He must be a caliph.*

"Paul," Eleanor calls out from the third row, "have the Sultan walk away when he says, 'He must be a caliph.' Then have him look over his shoulder on the last part of the line. Try it again."

He does.

"Perfect!"

The Sultan's command is now given. If Aladdin is to win the Princess, the Mother must take this order to him:

SULTAN: *I command your son to send me . . . uum . . . ten slaves . . . no, no . . . make that twenty . . . no, forty slaves, with trays of diamonds exactly like the ones you have brought here today. Each slave must lead a camel laden with jewels. Each camel must lead an elephant laden with jewels.*

Two minutes later there is a thunderous din from the refrigerator box. A cascade of sheer red fabric spills over the stage, topped by the glistening gold face of the Djinn, his head wrapped in a red jeweled turban. His jet black, beaded eyes flash under the stage lights. Fully extended, the Djinn dwarfs Aladdin, the stage, the audience. The puppet god has risen.

Within a minute, the caravan bearing the jewel-laden trays undulates across the floor in front of the puppet stage. The elephants, the camels, the slaves move in concert, for the swinging parts of the flat plywood cutouts have been linked with cord from behind. However, each figure has a characteristic movement depending on its shape. "Oh, darn!" Paul says just after the procession has crossed the floor and gone behind stage. "I broke an elephant's trunk."

It is a week before the premier performance of *Aladdin and His Wonderful Lamp*. The elephant's trunk has been repaired. Eleanor sits in the back of the theater.

"My finger can't do that, Eleanor!"

"Yes, it can, Paul."

"No, it can't."

"Fingers can do anything."

"They can't bend backward, at least not yet."

Paul and Eleanor are discussing the scene in which the Princess, after having been taken away by the Magician, pretends that she will marry him. The two puppets are seated on a small platform piled with miniature pillows. There is a small table nearby bearing a tiny bunch of grapes. "He must lean forward, Paul, in curiosity. Kind of scoop his head forward." Eleanor makes the gesture with her own head, but it is one of the most difficult ones to achieve with a puppet, for fingers do not flex backward. So, instead, Paul creates the illusion of the gesture by dipping the puppet's head slightly forward and turning it a fraction toward the audience.

It looks good. The Princess leaves to fetch a goblet of wine laced with the sleeping potion. The Magician jumps up and exclaims, *"I knew I would win her over!"* He laughs and swishes his cape. The cape hits the table. The small platform with the pillows, table, and grapes topples forward over the edge of the stage and hits the floor with a crash. Pillows scatter, grapes roll. "Oh, no!" moans a voice backstage. It is not the Princess's voice, the evil Magician's, or Aladdin's. It's Paul speaking. Just plain Paul.

It is two days before the performance. Dress rehearsal is about to begin. "Lights! Music!" calls Eleanor from the second row center.

Paul swirls out. His eyes tense under the turban. "I am al-Hariri," he exclaims a bit too shrilly. "A teller of tales, a spinner of dreams"—his tongue begins to trip slightly—"a sculptor with words. I'll tell you . . . ." He stops and stares blankly. "I forget what I'm going to tell you." Eleanor prompts him. He must be prompted several more times in that scene.

During the next hour, everything that could go wrong does. The curtain on Aladdin's house catches and pulls up to reveal Paul's face. Aladdin's legs tangle as he tries to sit. Paul forgets to change the scenery from city to desert. The Royal Herald's head is held much too far back. The Magician, swapping new lamps for old ones in his attempt to get Aladdin's, cannot get the new lamp out of the basket. *"Here, take the whole darn basket!"* he shouts and shoves it toward the Princess's Servant. A few minutes later Paul's voice wails from backstage, "I've lost a puppet! Darn! Where did that Sultan go? How can you do this to me? Where are you?"

Eleanor Boylan turns to Karen and John, who are also watching the rehearsal, and whispers, "Paul's disintegrating." She then turns back toward the stage. "It's okay, Paul. Typical dress rehearsal." The only thing that does not go wrong is that the platform with the pillows and grapes does not fall off. Paul has screwed hooks into the platform to secure it to the stage's edge. As an added precaution, a small piece of adhesive material has been glued on the wine goblet and a matching one on the spot on the table where it will rest, so there will be no surprise spills.

At 12:30 Paul breaks for lunch. The talk is lively. Eleanor and Karen and John eat hungrily and talk puppets and costumes and music. Paul says very little and mostly fiddles with a French fry on his plate.

PRESENTING ALADDIN AND HIS WONDERFUL LAMP

It is now Saturday, June 2, the day before the first performance of *Aladdin and His Wonderful Lamp*. Paul pushes thoughts of disastrous dress rehearsals from his mind. He gets up early and begins to pack up the show to transport it to the Danforth Museum in Framingham, Massachusetts, for its premier performance.

The puppets will be stacked into one large black suitcase, each in an individual plastic bag. This case will also hold some of the scenery, the Princess's bathhouse, and Aladdin's house. There are two long, narrow boxes. One contains the stage lights, and the other curtains for the stage. Tucked away in the various folds of the curtains are innumerable props—the magic lamp, bags of gold, chests of jewels, goblets, the small pillows for the platform scene. Also in this box is the trick Dwarf puppet that turns into the evil Magician, which is too long to fit into the suitcase with the other puppets. Two smaller cases contain extension cords, various tools, dimmers for lights, and rolls of tape. Finally, there are several large plastic bags that hold the flats, larger pieces of scenery, and the Djinn, folded up neatly to the size of a scatter pillow.

All of these cases, including the pieces of Paul's collapsible stage, fit into the back of his station wagon. By midmorning Paul is packed and heading out on Route 9 toward Framingham, which is about twenty miles outside of Boston.

By midafternoon he is set up, and by six o'clock that evening he is in the middle of a run-through of the show. Just as the Sultan is threatening to cut off Aladdin's head if the lost Princess is not found, the museum's custodian walks into the theater and says it's closing time.

Backstage, just beneath the stage floor, is a ledge, and under the ledge are thirteen hooks, one for each puppet to hang from as it awaits its cue. The props are lined up neatly on the ledge, and on the floor are larger pieces of scenery. Everything is ordered and arranged logically in terms of the action of the script and where it is easiest for Paul to reach. Doors are slamming now in the museum. The custodian is turning off the lights and turning on the alarm systems. Paul has just hung up the "poor" Aladdin puppet between the "rich" Aladdin and the Magician. The Sultan is on a hook to the extreme right between his daughter, the Princess, and the marionette of Aladdin mounted on his horse. Paul pushes his glasses back on his head, rubs his eyes briefly, and thinks that he will rehearse that opening speech on the drive back to Boston. He picks up his raincoat and glances at the semicircle of thirteen puppets hanging upside down. "Good night," he says, and walks out.

All through the night and into the morning the puppets will hang silent and still. They are without voice or life, just bundles of exquisitely sewn fabric awaiting the hand of the puppeteer who will give them movement, words, and passion.

It is June 3, 1:58 P.M. Within two minutes, a special kind of magic will begin. The children and their parents have been streaming into the theater at the Danforth Museum for twenty minutes.

The lights go down. Children grow still. One hugs her doll, another leans slightly forward on his mother's lap. There is a jangle of tambourines from behind stage and out sweeps al-Hariri—the teller of tales, the spinner of dreams, the sculptor with words. . . .

DJINN: *What is it you wish, Master? I am the Djinn of the Lamp. Ask for anything you want, for I must obey whoever rubs the lamp.*

MOTHER: *Look at us, Aladdin. We have always been poor. Already our friends and neighbors are surprised to see us so richly dressed. Be patient, my son. We will get rich* ___ *slowly.*

PRINCESS: *No one is allowed to look at me. My father, the Sultan, has forbidden it. You will lose your head.*

PRINCESS: *I think I know what wicked magic it is. Here*

MAGICIAN: *Come, my Princess, embrace me.*
PRINCESS: *First, let us drink some wine to seal the bargain.*

PRINCESS: *It worked. Aladdin, Aladdin!*

ALADDIN: *Good, now to get the lamp.*

PRINCESS: *It is under his cloak, there!*

ALADDIN: *The Djinn will imprison the magician and take us safely back to Bagdad.*

The house lights come up. Children applaud and crowd backstage, surrounding Paul.

"How did you turn the Dwarf into a Magician?"

"Where did you get those jewels?"

"Can I touch the horse?"

"Did the Sultan let Aladdin's Mother out of the dungeon after the Princess was found?"

The children are popping out their questions faster than Paul can answer them.

"But where are all the other people?" one child asks.

"What other people?" Paul says, looking down at the small girl who is staring directly up at him.

"The other people who said all those things."

Paul understands immediately.

"*You mean the other voices? Where did they all go?*" he says, speaking in the quick, silly voice of the Royal Herald. "Well, guess what? I can speak like the evil Magician, too." His voice is suddenly harsh. " *'I will get the lamp,'* " he barks. " *'Beware, Aladdin, I will destroy you!'* " The little girl moves back half a step. His voice softens. "I can speak like the Princess, too. *'No one is allowed to look at me,'* " he says, just as the Princess has spoken the words to Aladdin when they first met. " *'My father has forbidden it; that's why the Herald was here just a minute ago.'* " His voice shifts and becomes the Royal Herald's again. " *'Everyone inside! Everyone inside! The Princess goes to her baths!'* "

The children look up at Paul and stare at his mouth from which all the different voices have come. A few look at his hands and fingers.

"All those voices are just you?" asks a small boy, touching his sleeve.

"Just me," says Paul as he untwists the cloth horse's reins, and hangs the Sultan upside down. "Just me."